NAPLAN* Skills Handbook

*This is not an officially endorsed publication of the NAPLAN program and is produced by Amba Press independently of Australian governments

YEAR 7 TESTS PREPARATION GUIDE

7

I0374814

Published in 2025 by Amba Press, Melbourne, Australia
www.ambapress.com.au

© Kilbaha Education 2025

This is not an officially endorsed publication of the NAPLAN program and is produced by Amba Press independently of Australian governments.

All rights reserved. No part of this book may be reproduced or transmitted in any form or by any means, electronic or mechanical, including photocopying, recording or by any information storage and retrieval system, without prior permission in writing from the publisher.

Cover design: Tess McCabe
Editor: Rica Dearman

ISBN: 9781923215948 (pbk)
ISBN: 9781923215955 (ebk)

A catalogue record for this book is available from the National Library of Australia.

Contents

Introduction	1
What to expect	3
Revising for NAPLAN	5
Using this book	7
Test days tips	9
Writing test	11
Reading test	17
Language conventions test	39
Numeracy non-calculator test	53
Numeracy calculator test	64
Answers	75

Introduction

What is NAPLAN?

NAPLAN (National Assessment Program – Literacy and Numeracy) is a national test that all Australian students in Years 3, 5, 7 and 9 take each year. Think of it as a way to check how well you're doing with important skills like reading, writing and maths.

What is the purpose of NAPLAN?

NAPLAN helps you, your parents and your teachers understand how you're progressing with these essential skills. It's like a checkpoint to make sure you're on track with your learning and to identify any areas where you might need extra support.

What is being assessed?

NAPLAN tests four main areas:
- Writing (either a narrative or persuasive piece)
- Reading comprehension
- Language conventions (spelling, grammar and punctuation)
- Numeracy (maths and problem-solving)

How is it graded?

Your answers are marked either electronically (for multiple choice) or by trained markers (for writing and text entries). The tests are designed to adjust to your level – if you do well, you'll get harder questions; if you find them tricky, you'll get questions better matched to your level.

What results are provided?

You'll get a detailed report showing how you performed in each area. It shows your individual achievement and how you compare to other students in your year level across Australia.

Why is NAPLAN important?

NAPLAN is important for schools, the government and education planning, but for you personally, it's just one test on one day – it won't affect your grades, high school graduation or future opportunities, so try your best, but don't stress too much about it.

What to expect?

What tests are involved?

You'll complete four different tests:
- Writing
- Reading
- Language conventions
- Numeracy (with both calculator and non-calculator sections)

Why is NAPLAN online?

The online format makes the tests more personalised to your ability level. It's also faster to get results and includes helpful features like being able to flag questions to review later.

When, what and how?

- Tests happen at school in March
- You'll use a computer or tablet
- Each test has a different time limit
- You can use tools like calculators (in certain sections), rulers and protractors when needed
- You can flag questions to come back to later

How does the timer work in NAPLAN online?

The test screen shows a timer that counts down how much time is left. You can choose to hide or show this timer during most of the test, but in the last five minutes, the timer will automatically appear to let you know time is nearly up.

How do audio parts of the test work?

You'll need headphones for some parts of the test, especially for spelling questions and maths problems. The test includes audio that reads out the writing task and maths questions to help you understand them better.

Revising for NAPLAN

Why revise for NAPLAN?

Practising helps you feel more confident and comfortable with the test format. When you're familiar with the types of questions, you can focus on showing what you know rather than worrying about how the test works.

How to revise?

There are many ways to revise. Try some of these:
- Practise similar questions
- Get familiar with the online format using the public demonstration site
- Review topics you find challenging
- Try different question types
- Practise managing your time
- Conduct trial tests

Why do trial tests?

Trial tests help you:
- Get used to the test format
- Practise time management
- Identify areas where you might need more practice
- Feel more confident on test day

Do the tests in this book match those in NAPLAN online?

The questions are similar in style and difficulty to what you'll see in NAPLAN, but remember that the actual online test will adjust to your performance level as you go.

Using this book

How is this book organised?

Each section focuses on one test area (writing, reading, language or numeracy) and includes:

- Practise questions
- Example answers
- Tips and strategies
- Explanations of different question types

Each student in Australia takes the NAPLAN tests in the same order:

Day 1: Writing

Day 2: Reading

Day 3: Conventions of language (grammar, punctuation, spelling)

Day 4: Numeracy

Session 1: Non-calculator

Session 2: Calculator-allowed

How should you use this book?

There are many ways you can use it:

- Start with areas you find most challenging
- Complete the practise tests under timed conditions
- Review your answers and understand any mistakes
- Use the online practise tests to get familiar with the computer format
- Take breaks between practise sessions
- Keep track of topics you need to review more

Test days tips

How to prepare for test days?

Here are some other ways you can prepare for the NAPLAN tests:

- Get a good sleep the night before
- Have a healthy breakfast
- Arrive at school on time
- Bring your water bottle
- Make sure you have the equipment you need (like headphones)
- Download and install the NAPLAN Locked Down browser
- Go to the toilet before the test starts
- Take some slow, deep breaths to stay calm

What happens if you are sick on one of the test days?

Don't worry! If you're sick on test day, stay home and get better. Your school will arrange for you to do the test on another day during the NAPLAN test window. There are catch-up tests available for students who are absent during the main testing period.

What happens if you don't feel you did well on the day?

Remember that NAPLAN is just one test on one day – it's not a pass or fail test. Everyone has good days and bad days. Your teachers look at lots of different ways to assess how you're going at school, not just NAPLAN. If you're worried about your performance, talk to your parents or teachers about it. They can help explain your results when they arrive and provide support if needed.

Stressed? Nervous? Anxious?

Here are some techniques you could use if you feel stressed or nervous during the actual test:

- Take slow, deep breaths – breathe in for four counts, hold for four, breathe out for four
- Remember you can flag difficult questions and come back to them later
- Have a quick stretch in your chair
- Take a sip of water
- Close your eyes for a moment if you need to
- Focus on one question at a time rather than thinking about the whole test
- Remind yourself that you've prepared well and are doing your best
- Use positive self-talk like *I can do this* or *I'll try my best*

Writing test

You have 60 minutes to complete the writing test.

You will be provided with a 'writing stimulus' or 'prompt' – an idea or topic – and asked to write a response of a particular text type (genre).

In the actual NAPLAN test you will write a narrative OR a persuasive piece of writing.

We have provided one test example of each style and some suggestions to keep in mind for each one.

You are to type your answer online but can prepare or plan your response with a pen/pencil and paper.

Marking criteria

Based on the marking guides, here are the 10 criteria you will be assessed on for both persuasive and narrative writing:

1. Audience – the writer's capacity to orient, engage and affect the reader
2. Text structure – the organisation of structural components into an effective text structure
    - For narrative: orientation, complication and resolution
    - For persuasive: introduction, body and conclusion
3. Ideas – the creation, selection and crafting of ideas
4. Content focus
    - For narrative: character and setting (development of character and sense of place/time)
    - For persuasive: persuasive devices (use of devices to enhance the writer's position)
5. Vocabulary – the range and precision of language choices
6. Cohesion – the control of multiple threads and relationships across the text using referring words, substitutions, word associations and text connectives
7. Paragraphing – the segmenting of text into paragraphs that assists the reader
8. Sentence structure – the production of grammatically correct, structurally sound and meaningful sentences
9. Punctuation – the use of correct and appropriate punctuation to aid reading of the text
10. Spelling – the accuracy of spelling and the difficulty of the words used

Writing a strong narrative piece

Your narrative writing will be assessed across 10 key areas. Here's what examiners are looking for:

Structure and organisation

- Start with a clear orientation that sets up your characters and situation
- Develop a complication or problem that creates tension
- Build to an effective resolution that wraps up the story
- Don't just end with 'it was all a dream' or 'they lived happily ever after'
- Use paragraphs to organise different parts of your story

Creating engaging characters and settings

- Bring characters to life through their actions, thoughts, feelings and dialogue
- Show rather than tell: instead of 'She was sad', write 'Tears rolled down her cheeks as she turned away'
- Create atmosphere through descriptive details about the setting
- Help readers visualise the scene through specific sensory details
- Develop the relationship between characters

Vocabulary and language

- Choose precise words that create vivid images: 'prowled' instead of 'walked'
- Use figurative language like similes and metaphors thoughtfully
- Include dialogue that sounds natural and reveals character
- Vary your word choices to maintain reader interest

The River

Today you are going to write a story.

The title for your story is 'The River'.

Your story might be about any adventure, crossing a river or travelling on a river.

It could be about a place close to a river where something important happens.

Your story could be about people who live near a river. They may be helped by the river or put in danger by it.

Think about:

- The characters and where they are
- The complications or problems to be solved
- How the story will end

Remember to:

- Plan your story before you start
- Write in sentences
- Pay attention to the words you choose, your spelling and punctuation
- Check and edit your story when you have finished

Writing a strong persuasive piece

Your persuasive writing will be assessed across 10 key areas. Here's what examiners are looking for:

Vocabulary and spelling

Choose your words carefully to show sophisticated expression. Include:

- Precise words that strengthen your argument (for example, 'essential', 'beneficial', 'crucial')
- Challenging words used correctly (for example, 'environment', 'consequently', 'responsibility')
- Difficult words that demonstrate range (for example, 'evaluate', 'significant', 'analyse')
- Remember: it's better to spell simpler words correctly than to attempt challenging words incorrectly.

Sentence structure

Vary your sentences to create impact:

- Use simple sentences for emphasis: 'Animals deserve better'
- Create complex sentences to show relationships between ideas: 'Although some people argue that zoos protect animals, the restricted environment damages their wellbeing'
- Avoid run-on sentences: Instead of 'Animals need space they need freedom they need care', write 'Animals need space, freedom and proper care'
- Watch for comma splices: Instead of 'Zoos can be cruel, they restrict animal movement', write 'Zoos can be cruel because they restrict animal movement'

Every student should play a sport.

Do you agree?

Do you disagree?

Perhaps you can think of ideas for both sides.

Write to convince a reader of your opinion.

- **Start with an introduction.** An introduction lets a reader know what you are going to write about.

- **Write your opinion on the topic.** Give reasons for your opinion. Explain your reasons.

- **Finish with a conclusion.** A conclusion sums up your reasons so that a reader is convinced of your opinion.

Remember to:

- Plan your writing
- Use paragraphs to organise your ideas
- Write in sentences
- Choose your words carefully to convince a reader of your opinion
- Pay attention to your spelling and punctuation
- Check and edit your writing so that it is clear for a reader

Reading test

This is a reading test.

There are 41 questions.

You have 65 minutes to complete the reading test.

In this test you will need to read each text, then read each question and choose the correct answer.

Read *Australian drought* and then answer questions 1 to 6.

Australian drought

15 June

Dear Editor,

Our country is experiencing the worst drought in its history. Farmers are struggling to keep their crops and their livestock alive. We need to manage our water resources as carefully as possible and treat water like it is gold, before it all runs out.

It makes me so angry when I see people wasting water, using it to wash things like the outsides of their houses or their cars when they should be using grey water from their washing machines to do these things. Better yet, they should be using rainwater tanks.

I don't think the Government is doing enough. I think the Government should provide every house in Australia with a water tank, so that every household can use rainwater wherever they can instead of using precious drinking water from their taps for everything.

We all need to be more conscious of our environment.

Patty Wilkins

22 June

Dear Editor,

I agree with Patty Wilkins' letter (15 June) in that all Australians need to be conserving water and that we need to be conscious of our environment.

I don't think she has a right to be angry at people, though. People pay a lot of money for their cars and cars need to be washed so that they can be protected from damaging bird droppings that can eat away at the paint. But I do agree that recycled water and rainwater should be used.

Our Government has put plenty of restrictions on the use of water such as only allowing people to water plants two days per week and only prior to eight o'clock in the morning.

Also, anyone who buys a rainwater tank can claim money back from the Government to cover some of the costs.

I also don't think there are many people being water 'Wallys'. Most people are doing their best to save water wherever they can.

Bill Freedman

Australian drought questions 1 to 6.

1. **Where does grey water come from?**
   - ○ taps
   - ○ rainwater tanks
   - ○ washing machines
   - ○ gutters

2. **Which of the following do the two writers disagree on?**
   - ○ water needs to be conserved
   - ○ the Government is doing enough
   - ○ the environment is precious
   - ○ rainwater tanks help in a drought

3. **Bill writes that the Government has *'put plenty of restrictions on the use of water'*. Why does he write this?**
   - ○ he agrees with Patty
   - ○ he works for the Government
   - ○ he disagrees with Patty
   - ○ he thinks that Australians are water 'Wallys'

4. **Why does Patty think that water tanks are a great idea?**
   - ○ so people will use less grey water
   - ○ so people will use more tap water
   - ○ so people can get money back from the Government
   - ○ so people will use more rainwater

5. **What does Patty's letter tell us about Patty?**
    - that she likes the Government
    - that she cares for the environment
    - that she cares for Bill
    - that she is not a farmer

6. **What type of letter is Bill's?**
    - a comment
    - an instruction
    - a response
    - a list

Read *Eggs* and then answer questions 7 to 12.

Eggs

By Aoife Bearsley

Thomas isn't back with the eggs yet, but my feet are burning, so I lay the towel out next to the tin on the concrete and sit in the middle of it. I want to be in the shade but Thomas reckons the tin has to be in the full sun.

It will get hot enough. The sun is about as close to the Earth as it can get on days like today. It's like a big orange ball up there and down here everything is tinged with yellow. All the leaves on the trees kind of sparkle and those 'birches' Mum loves so much look a bit sick on days like today, with the tops of them tipping over toward the ground like they're looking for something to drink.

The back door squeaks and a few seconds later Thomas tiptoes down the drive, staying in the strip of shade next to the house. 'They're straight from the fridge,' he whispers, 'so they should sizzle really well.'

'Was your dad up?' I ask, but I know he wasn't because Thomas wouldn't have gone inside for the eggs if his dad was awake. He would have snuck up back to the chook shed instead.

'No. He did a late shift last night, so I reckon it should be at least three o'clock before I have to go in.' Thomas sits and grins, drawing two speckled eggs out from his pocket and places them down between us on the towel.

He splays his hand out over the tin lid, not touching it, but very close. He presses a fingertip down on the lid and then rips his hand back toward his chest. 'Wow, mate!' he cackles, 'that feels hot enough to cook a steak on!' He inspects his finger and shows it to me. It's bright red on the tip. I laugh. He plucks an egg from the towel and I do the same. We sit grinning at one another for a moment, holding our eggs next to the rim of the tin.

Thomas counts to three and we both crack our eggs, splitting their hard bellies open and pouring their guts out onto the lid. The eggs slide and wobble a bit, but their clear jelly bodies start to turn a wispy, milky white…

Eggs questions 7 to 12.

7. **Why would Thomas have gone up to the chook shed instead of the house?**

    o   to get out of the sun

    o   because his dad wouldn't catch him stealing eggs from there

    o   to hide from the narrator

    o   for extra eggs

8. **What does the narrator mean by the sentence '...*It will get hot enough*'?**

    _____

    _____

9. **What does '...*their clear jelly bodies start to turn a wispy, milky white...*' mean?**

    o   Thomas and the narrator are turning white

    o   the sun is going down

    o   the eggs are cooking

    o   the eggs are rotten

10. **In the story, Thomas' dad did a late shift the night before, so Thomas thinks he has until at least three o'clock before he has to go in. This suggests that Thomas**

    o   needs to go in before the sun goes down

    o   needs to go in before his dad wakes up

    o   knows that his dad will not be angry

    o   will get into trouble if he goes to the chook shed

11. **What kind of word best describes the relationship between Thomas and the narrator?**
    - brothers
    - enemies
    - friends
    - cousins

12. **Why do you think the narrator laughs when Thomas shows off his burnt finger?**
    - because he is hot
    - because he wants Thomas to be hurt
    - because he doesn't like Thomas
    - because he is amazed

Read *Water baby* and then answer questions 13 to 18.

Water baby

By Kirsty Murray

When the starting gun went off, Shane cut the water like a knife. She knew she was swimming well – she felt light and smooth. The water seemed to rush past beneath her. All her movements were precise, her arm stroke exact and powerful. The other competitors didn't have a chance. She took the lead and held it for the entire race.

When Shane climbed out of the pool and mounted the podium to receive her gold medal, she became the youngest Australian Olympic medallist in history. She was 15 years old…

Shane Elizabeth Gould was born in Sydney on 23 November 1956. She loved the water from babyhood. When bathtime was over, she cried to get back in the water. Before she was three she could swim underwater at the pool with her eyes open, and at five she was snorkelling around the reefs of Fiji. By the time she was 15 years old, she held every women's world freestyle record from 100 m to 1,500 m.

Shane had the perfect physique for a swimmer – tall and slim with wide shoulders and narrow hips. By the time she was 13, she knew that her gift for swimming was something special – she gave up all other interests and gave herself over to competitive swimming. She set her alarm for early-morning training, watched her diet and kept a logbook of her training routines. Her persistence and single-mindedness paid off. Between April 1971 and January 1972, she set seven new world records. By July 1972, she was so confident that she'd win gold at the Games that she asked her parents if she could have her braces removed just for the competition. She knew the cameras would be flashing and she wanted to look her best.

Shane Gould won three gold, one silver and a bronze medal at the 1972 Olympics.

Water baby questions 13 to 18.

13. **When the starting gun went off, Shane *'cut the water like a knife'*. This means that Shane**
    - used a knife to cut the water
    - dove into the water roughly
    - went through the water sharply
    - swam very slowly

14. **The text states that Shane *'gave herself over to competitive swimming'.* This means that she**
    - gave up going to school
    - gave up her diet
    - brought herself over to the swimming pool
    - gave up other activities for swimming

15. **Shane swam open-eyed underwater**
    - during bathtime
    - by age three
    - while snorkelling
    - by age five

16. **The main purpose of this text is to**
    - instruct
    - criticise
    - argue
    - inform

17. **Which quote from the text best shows that Shane was very determined to succeed?**
    - ○ *'she knew her gift for swimming was special'*
    - ○ *'she was so confident she'd win'*
    - ○ *'her persistence and single-mindedness paid off'*
    - ○ *'she loved the water from babyhood'*

18. **Why did Shane ask for her braces to be removed before the Olympics?**
    - ○ because they were slowing her down
    - ○ because she was confident she was going to win
    - ○ because she didn't like her photo being taken
    - ○ because she was persistent

Read *The birds have come back* and then answer questions 19 to 24.

The birds have come back

By Joan Boundy

They came back this morning – four days after the bushfires of Ash Wednesday had devastated our small village of Upper Beaconsfield. From our mountaintop I saw them – flocks of starlings swaying in the thermal in the valley below, white cockatoos screeching and rosellas leaping with joy as they found green foliage that escaped the flames. Small honeyeaters picked busily at the tree trunks and a lone kookaburra laughed hollowly as he sat on a charred fence post.

It is four days since we fled the flames that spread mercilessly as the north wind roared around us. Everything now had a nightmare quality about it – you feel you will wake up and everything will be bright and beautiful and new again; but it is no nightmare – the charred remains of church, store, garage and numerous homes are grim evidence of reality.

The Birds Have Come Back questions 19 to 24.

19. **What do you think the writer is trying to show when she describes the kookaburra as laughing 'hollowly'?**
    - ○ the kookaburra sounded hollow from far away
    - ○ the hollow joy of the fires being over
    - ○ the kookaburra was lonely
    - ○ how hot it was

20. **What does the birds' coming back represent?**

    _____

    _____

21. **What word best describes the birds in the first paragraph?**
    - ○ sad
    - ○ devastated
    - ○ hopeful
    - ○ elated

22. **How does the tone of the piece change in the second paragraph?**

    _____

    _____

23. **Which of the following sentences in the passage best shows the writer's sense of helplessness?**
    - ○ *'white cockatoos screeching'*
    - ○ *'flames that spread mercilessly'*
    - ○ *'they had escaped the flames'*
    - ○ *'the north wind roared'*

24. **What does *'swaying in the thermal'* mean?**
    - the birds were cooling down
    - the birds were drifting in the heat
    - the valley was barren
    - the birds were being baked

Read the children's non-fiction book review: *Ned Kelly: Black Snake* by Carole Wilkinson and then answer questions 25 to 29.

The daring of Ned Kelly – book review

By Sally Murphy

Ned Kelly was only 25 years old when he died. Yet within his short life he came to prominence as a thief, a bank robber and a murderer. In the 122 since his death, he has been portrayed in books, films and in art. Why has he remained such a prominent figure in Australia's history?

Black Snake: The Daring of Ned Kelly offers insight into the life of the outlaw and the chain of events which led to his hanging. In clear, easy-to-understand language, author Carole Wilkinson recounts Kelly's life from birth to his final moments. She details his criminal activities and his life on the run, his family connections and his friendships, giving the reader a detailed idea of the man and his motives.

Each chapter opens with a fictionalised recount from one of the characters present at the various events in Kelly's life, and the text is supported by archival photographs, press clippings and quotes from correspondence and other documents.

This is not a glorification of a criminal career – it is instead a historical exploration of the man who was Ned Kelly, and an exploration of why he chose to lead the life he did. Wilkinson challenges the reader to make their own decision as to whether Kelly was a villain or a hero, a rebel or simply misunderstood.

Author Carole Wilkinson was born in England and came to Australia as a teenager. Writing about history is her passion. Her other titles include the *Ramose* series, set in Ancient Egypt.

Black Snake: The Daring of Ned Kelly by Carole Wilkinson, Black Dog Books, 2002

Children's non-fiction book review: *Ned Kelly: Black Snake* questions 25 to 29.

25. **In *Ned Kelly: Black Snake*, why might the author have opened each chapter with a *'fictionalised recount'*?**
    - ○ it shows Ned Kelly as the terrible villain he was
    - ○ to tell the *story* of Ned Kelly as well as the *history* of Ned Kelly
    - ○ there was not enough accurate information available
    - ○ it allows the reader to make their own decisions

26. **Which sentence best suggests that *Ned Kelly: Black Snake* reveals more about Ned Kelly than other books about the outlaw?**
    - ○ '*...supported by archival photographs*'
    - ○ '*...offers insight into the life of the outlaw*'
    - ○ '*...recounts Kelly's life from his birth*'
    - ○ '*...quotes from correspondence*'

27. **'*This is not a glorification of a criminal career*' – what does this mean?**

    _____

    _____

28. **The *main* purpose of this review is to**
    - ○ inform the reader about Ned Kelly's history
    - ○ inform the reader about the author, Carole Wilkinson
    - ○ recommend *Black Snake* for reading
    - ○ explain that this book is different from other histories of Ned Kelly

29. **This review is**
    - a criticism
    - an argument
    - a comment
    - an analysis

Read *Should we abolish zoos?* and then answer questions 30 to 36.

Should we abolish zoos?

JaneyB   6.21 pm

We should definitely abolish zoos. It's not fair to keep animals in such small spaces that are nothing like their real habitats. This is especially true for marine animals that don't have enough water to swim around in. The cages at the zoo are really restrictive and confined.

Spaceman   6.32 pm

The zoos of today are nothing like the zoos of old. Especially in countries like Australia. There are many very good zoos that have created natural surroundings for their animals, with plenty of foliage to take shelter and space to roam around.

Big Brother   6.40 pm

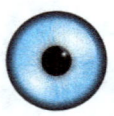

Zoos play a really important part in the survival of endangered species. There are many animals whose natural habitats are being destroyed and are in danger of becoming extinct. Having zoos where these species can be kept alive and where research can be carried out to help them survive is vital.

Johnno   6.43 pm

Zoos are heavily regulated by laws that prohibit any cruelty to animals. Plus they are a great educational resource for people.

JaneyB   6.48 pm

The best way to learn about animals is to observe them in their own habitat in the wild, not in some manufactured setting that humans have made for them. It gives an artificial impression of the animals' behaviours because they are not in a natural setting.

Spaceman   6.50 pm

Again, most zoos do a great job of creating a realistic environment for the animals they keep. Open-range zoos are particularly good at this. The only difference is that the animals are safer in these zoos than they are in their natural habitats because there are no predators.

Should we abolish zoos? questions 30 to 36.

30. What is Big Brother's main argument?
- ○ animals make an important contribution to education
- ○ animals are protected by laws on cruelty
- ○ modern zoos are animal friendly
- ○ zoos make an important contribution to species preservation

31. JaneyB refers to zoos as *'some manufactured setting'.* What is the tone of this argument?
- ○ joking
- ○ critical
- ○ practical
- ○ approving

32. What are they all likely to agree on?
- ○ modern zoos are different to zoos of old
- ○ animals should be protected
- ○ zoos are restricted by laws
- ○ all animals are better off in the wild

33. JaneyB argues that zoos give humans an *'artificial impression'.* What she means is that
- ○ animals in the wild are better off
- ○ only humans benefit from the existence of zoos
- ○ animals do not behave realistically in the zoo
- ○ animals in the zoo are artificial

34. **In her first comment, what is JaneyB's main concern?**
    - ○ zoos are not educational
    - ○ zoos are not realistic
    - ○ zoos keep animals away from their real homes
    - ○ zoos are environmentally unfriendly

35. **Spaceman argues that the only difference between zoo habitats and wild habitats is that *'there are no predators'*. This means that**
    - ○ zoos only keep animals that aren't predators
    - ○ zoos ensure that the animals can't hurt one another
    - ○ humans can view the animals safely
    - ○ wild habitats are better

36. **What effect might this lack of predators have on the animals?**

    _____

    _____

Read *Greetings from Luanda, Angola* and answer questions 37 to 41.

Greetings from Luanda, Angola

The story so far...

During our 16 months here we've seen much change in Luanda. There's a greater variety of goods for sale and an election, the first for nearly two decades, has brought some hope. The roads are being widened and resealed, the parks are undergoing landscaping and traffic lights are being installed and maintained. Armies of workers (mainly Chinese) toil in the sun, chiselling cubes of stone to fashion patterned footpaths. New hotels are going up, churches are being restored, clinics built and the once beautiful fort that sits above the city is having a facelift.

Of course the traffic is still horrendous, the national airline is still considered a risky ride and most of the population still lives in shanties without running water or a reliable electricity supply. The people remain friendly, polite and good-natured, but many are desperately poor.

'Amiga! Amiga!' cries the lady in the street. 'Ananas?' She points to the pineapples carried in a huge basket on her head. I think of the two pineapples I've just bought in the market and am about to walk on. Then I see a tiny child strapped to her back and her round stomach just starting to show a baby bump. I buy a pineapple, take it home and give it to the guard.

Christmas in Luanda is a colourful time and this year there seems to be more trees, decorations and 'things to buy' than there were last year. The powers that be have erected a huge tree placed in front of the President's mother's house and several more along major roads. Large orange-flowered jacarandas add splashes of colour to an otherwise drab-grey cement city.

To be continued...

Greetings from Luanda, Angola questions 37 to 41

37. **In the first paragraph, Luanda is portrayed as**
    - o a desolate landscape
    - o a place undergoing development
    - o a large, bustling city
    - o a drab-grey cement city

38. **Why do you think the third paragraph is written in the form of a story?**
    - o so that the writing does not become monotonous
    - o to ensure that the reader is concentrating
    - o to make the scene shorter
    - o to show the reader how the poverty in Luanda affects the writer

39. *'...this year there seems to be more trees, decorations and "things to buy" than there were last year.'* **What does this suggest?**
    - o Christmas is becoming more popular in Luanda
    - o the President's mother likes Christmas trees
    - o Luanda is becoming more prosperous
    - o the writer is beginning to like Luanda

40. *'There's greater variety of goods for sale and an election, the first for nearly two decades, has brought some hope.'* **What might they be hoping for?**

    ○ less poverty

    ○ to leave Luanda

    ○ more Christmas merchandise

    ○ more markets

41. **Why does the writer change her mind and buy a pineapple?**

    _____

    _____

Language conventions test

This is the language conventions test (which covers spelling, grammar and punctuation).

There are 50 questions.

You have 50 minutes to complete the language conventions test.

There will be a mix of question types including:

- Multiple choice
- Short answer
- Error identification/correction
- Fill in the blank/missing word

The test typically starts with spelling questions before moving into grammar and punctuation. You need to identify errors and show your understanding of correct language usage through these various question formats.

Spelling

Each sentence has one word that is incorrectly spelt. Write the correct spelling of the word in the box.

1. We need to show caushun when crossing the road.

2. I am very good at rapping presents.

3. The mountain's summit was at a great hite.

4. The art galery has many famous paintings.

5. Tim ran the cross-country course energeticly.

6. The tourist lost his luggidge at the airport.

7. The fan wanted the celebrity's autograf.

8. It is rude to talk with a mouthfull of food.

9. Sientists will soon discover a cure for cancer.

10. Professor Jones studied the dinosaur fossil.

11. The cathedral was visited as a holey shrine.

12. The hospital pashent was recovering from her injuries.

13. You will find my letter inclosed in the package.

14. It is important to do some streching before exercise.

The spelling mistakes in these sentences have been circled. Write the correct spelling for each circled word in the box.

15. Jack showed his (strenth) when he carried

16. that heavy sack of (potatos) all the way home.

17. Everyone comments on how (musculer)

18. he is, but it was still very (impresive.)

19. He appears so (distrest) every time

20. I make any (atempt) to

21. (approche) him that I'm not

22. sure how to (acheeve) it.

23. He wore a (disgize) that was

24. so (efective) that not even his

25. own family could (gess) who he was.

Grammar and punctuation

26. Which of the following correctly completes the sentence?

You can travel more _____ by train than you can by car.

quick	quicker	quickest	quickly
○	○	○	○

27. Which of the following correctly completes the sentence?

Dora went to bed early last night because she _____ tired.

have	is	was	were
○	○	○	○

28. Shade one bubble to show where the missing apostrophe (') should go.

Mark looked for the dogs lead so that his sisters could take the dog for a walk.
    ○   ○   ○   ○

29. Which of the following correctly completes the sentence?

Prince William, _____ is heir to the throne, is a good horse rider.

that	which	when	who
○	○	○	○

30. Which of the following correctly completes the sentence?

The book, _____ was green, belonged to the library.

who	what	which	why
○	○	○	○

31. Which sentence is correct?

○ I and Jane is very good at playing tennis.

○ Me and Jane are very good at playing tennis.

○ Jane and me is very good at playing tennis.

○ Jane and I are very good at playing tennis.

32. Which of the following correctly completes the sentence?

The use of herbs and spices in cooking _____ on the increase in Australia.

is	are	am	were
○	○	○	○

33. Which of the following correctly completes the sentences?

Karen is very tall. _____, her older brother is quite short.

So	Therefore	However	Because
○	○	○	○

34. Which sentence has the correct punctuation?

○ He asked for it politely, so I let him have it.

○ He asked "for it politely," so, I let him have it.

○ He asked for "it politely" so I let him, have it.

○ He asked, "for it politely, so I let him", have it.

35. Which of the following correctly completes the sentence?

They bought tickets that allowed them to sit the _____ to the stage.

more closest	closest	closely	more closer
○	○	○	○

36. Which of the following correctly completes the sentence?

The kangaroo and the koala are native _____ Australia.

for	with	in	to
○	○	○	○

37. Which of the following correctly completes the sentence?

They _____ driven slower in the rain.

should of	should'ave	should've	shouldve
○	○	○	○

38. Which of the following correctly completes the sentence?

The restaurant had an _____ atmosphere that attracted customers.

vibrant	warm	alluring	joyful
○	○	○	○

39. Shade **two** bubbles to show where the missing commas (,) should go.

I enjoy eating fish and chips and I enjoy eating chocolate

but I wouldn't enjoy eating them together.

40. Which sentence is correct?

○ They were gathering them up and sorting them into pairs.

○ They gathered them up and sorting them into pairs.

○ They were gathering them up and were sorted them into pairs.

○ They gathered them and sort them into pairs.

41. Which of the following correctly completes the sentence?

He drove the car _____.

extremely quickly	extreme quick	extreme quickly	extremely quick
○	○	○	○

42. Which of the following correctly completes the sentence?

> Madeline decided _____ a new laptop computer.

on buying	in buying	buying	to buying
○	○	○	○

43. Which of the following correctly completes the sentence?

> Some people prefer savoury food _____ sweet food.

from	than	to	for
○	○	○	○

44. Shade one bubble to show where the missing apostrophe (') should go.

The girls really admired Amys new shoes made from crocodile skins.

45. Which sentence has the correct punctuation?

- ○ Suddenly a large bird swooped down swallowed a bug and flew off.
- ○ Suddenly, a large bird swooped down, swallowed a bug, and flew off.
- ○ Suddenly a large bird, swooped down, swallowed a bug, and flew off.
- ○ Suddenly a large bird swooped down, swallowed a bug and, flew off.

46. Which sentence has the correct punctuation?

○ The bats' wings, all flapping together, sounded like thunder.

○ The bat's wings, all flapping together, sounded like thunder.

○ The bats, wings all flapping together sounded, like thunder.

○ The bats' wing's all flapping, together sounded like thunder.

47. Which sentence is correct?

○ Lucy and Anne were still hungry even though they had eaten lunch.

○ Lucy and Anne were still hungry even though she has eaten lunch.

○ Lucy and Anne are still hungry even though they eaten lunch.

○ Lucy and Anne is still hungry even though they had eaten lunch.

48. Which of the following correctly completes the sentence?

Do you have a table _____ can seat thirteen?

who	that	what	and
○	○	○	○

49. Which sentence has the correct punctuation?

   ○ My brother will be in New Zealand on christmas day.

   ○ my brother will be in New zealand on Christmas Day.

   ○ My Brother will be in New Zealand on Christmas Day.

   ○ My brother will be in New Zealand on Christmas Day.

50. Which sentence has the correct punctuation?

   ○ as she left for work Chloe called to Tegan, "See you later".

   ○ As she left for work, Chloe called to Tegan, "See you later".

   ○ As she left for work, Chloe called to Tegan "see you later".

   ○ As she left for work, chloe called to tegan, "see you later".

Numeracy non-calculator test

This is a numeracy non-calculator test.

You have 40 minutes to complete the non-calculator test. This test has 32 questions to complete.

You cannot use a calculator, but you can use pen and paper to work out things.

This test focuses on basic numerical calculations and mathematical thinking without tools.

Both the numeracy non-nalculator and numeracy calculator tests use similar mathematical concepts including:

- Number and algebra
- Measurement and geometry
- Statistics and probability

You will get a break between the two tests on the day, however, they will both be completed on the same day.

1. What is the missing number?

   $6 \times \boxed{?} = 9 \times 8$

2.

   A cone is glued to the top of a cylinder. How many **vertices** are there?

1	3	4	5
○	○	○	○

3. What is another way of writing 5^2?

5×5	5×2	5+5	2×2×2×2×2
○	○	○	○

4.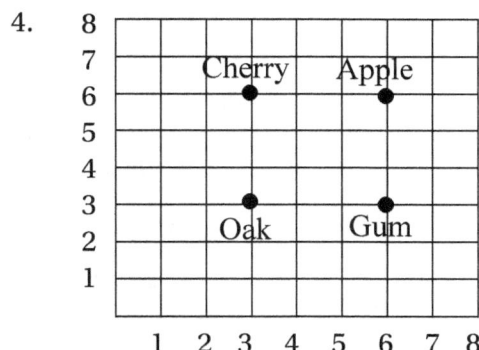

The above diagram shows where four trees are growing in a forest. Which tree is growing at (6, 3)?

Cherry	Apple	Oak	Gum
○	○	○	○

5. A box contains 15 black marbles and 1 white marble. Josie closes her eyes and selects a marble from the box. Which one of the following statements is true?

○ It is impossible for Josie to select a white marble.

○ It is likely that Josie will select a white marble.

○ It is unlikely that Josie will select a white marble.

○ It is certain that Josie will select a black marble.

6.

What is the time shown on the above clock ?

8:02	2:08	8:10	2:40
○	○	○	○

7. What is the missing number in the pattern?

   94 88 [?] 76

8. **X   M   W   P**

   Which one of the above letters does **not** have a line of symmetry?

X	M	W	P
○	○	○	○

9. What is 0.03 as a percentage?

10.

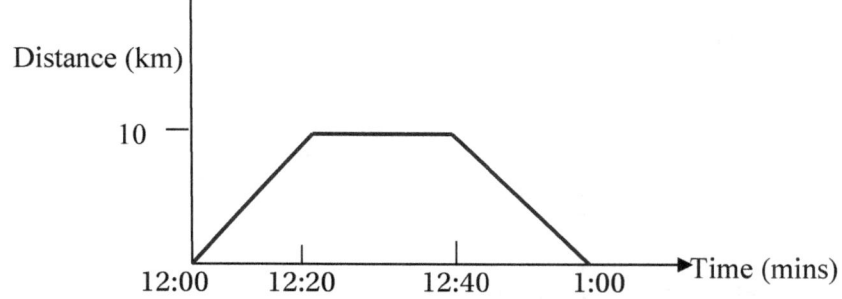

Amy left home at 12:00 noon and rode her bike to her friend's house. She then rode home again, arriving home at 1:00 pm. The above graph shows her journey. Which one of the following statements is true?

○ Amy stayed at her friend's house for 1 hour.

○ Amy took 40 minutes to reach her friend's house.

○ Amy took 20 minutes to ride home.

○ Amy rode home from her friend's house faster than she rode to her friend's house.

11.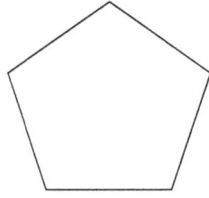

Each side of the above pentagonal fence is 40 m. A dog walks around the edge of this fence 5 times. How many metres has the dog walked?

12.

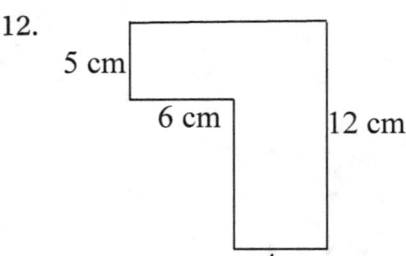

What is the perimeter of the above shape?

24cm	27cm	34cm	44cm
○	○	○	○

13. Which of the following numbers is the smallest?

1	1.02	1.1	1.2
○	○	○	○

14. If 3 cans of juice cost $6.45, then what is the cost of 2 cans of juice?

$

15. What is 526 rounded to the nearest 10?

16. What is $\frac{3}{8}$ of 24?

17. Jess walked from her home to her friend's house and arrived at 4:15. If it took Jess 25 minutes to walk this distance, then what time did she leave home?

3:05	3:45	3:50	3:55
○	○	○	○

18.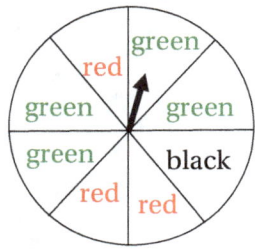

If the spinner above is spun once, then what is the chance of it pointing to green?

1:2	4:3	3:4	4:4
○	○	○	○

19. What does 2 × 3 + (8 − 5) ÷ 3 equal?

3	6	7	8
○	○	○	○

20. $60 is divided between Anne and Ben so that Anne gets three times as much money as Ben.

How much money does Ben get?

$ _____

21. Which mixed number has the same value as $\frac{33}{22}$?

$1\frac{2}{33}$	$1\frac{3}{22}$	$1\frac{1}{2}$	$2\frac{1}{11}$
○	○	○	○

22.

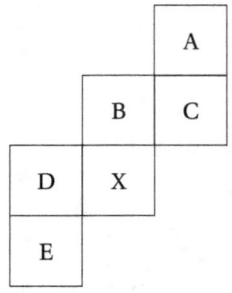

The above net is made into a cube.

What is the name of the face opposite the face named **X**?

A	C	D	E
○	○	○	○

23. Meg's home is the same distance from A as it is from B. Meg walks north-west to A from her home, and then east to B. In what direction does she need to walk from B in order to go directly home?

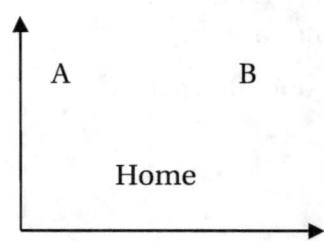

south-east	south-west	north-east	north-west
○	○	○	○

24.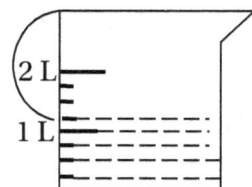

If Lynn adds 35 ml of liquid to the water in the above jug, how many litres of liquid will then be in the jug?

1.6	1.285	1.35	2.35
○	○	○	○

25. The reflex angle ABC 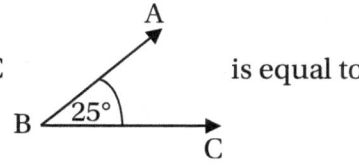 is equal to

145°	155°	335°	345°
○	○	○	○

26. John used $1\frac{1}{2}$ kg of fruit in a large cake.

He used $1\frac{3}{5}$ kg of sultanas, $\frac{1}{10}$ kg of currants and the remainder of the fruit was raisins. How many kilograms of raisins did he use?

27. The table below shows the results of a survey on faults in a company's computers, and the cost of repairs.

Age of computer	$150 or more	Greater than $100 and less than $150	$100 or less
Less than 2 years	3	5	6
2 to 5 years	10	9	12
More than 5 years	20	25	32

For this company, how many of their computers that were more than 5 years old had a repair cost of less than $150?

28. A maths test had a total of 50 marks. Finn got 76% for this test. How many marks did he get on the test?

29.

Alex, Bridie and Con are running towards a tree. Bridie is 9 metres from the tree, Con is 6 metres behind Alex, and 11 metres from the tree. How far is Bridie behind Alex?

metres

30. What is the answer to 8.4 ÷ 0.4?

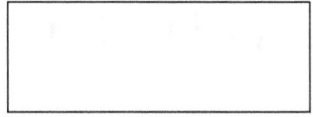

31. If 2 oranges weigh the same as 3 apples and 3 apricots weigh the same as 1 orange, then how many apricots weigh the same as 1 apple?

32.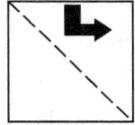

A square piece of paper has an arrow painted on it as shown in the above diagram. The paper is immediately folded along the dotted line, and an imprint of the arrow is made. When the paper is unfolded, what will it look like?

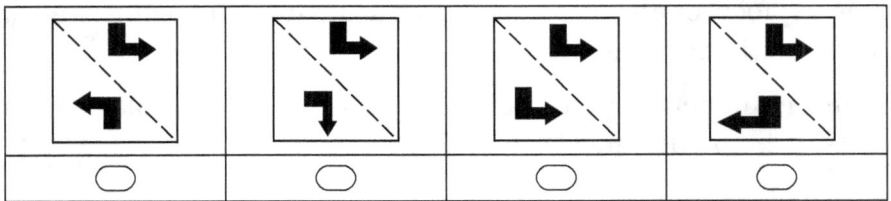

Numeracy calculator test

This is a numeracy calculator test.

You have 40 minutes to complete the numeracy calculator test.

This test has 32 questions to complete.

For your NAPLAN numeracy test, you'll have to use the calculator that's built into the test – you can't bring your own. This online calculator might feel a bit different from what you use in class, so here's a tip: practise using it before test day so you're comfortable with how it works. That way, you won't waste time during the test trying to figure out how it works. Remember, it's just a basic scientific calculator with standard functions, so once you've played around with it a bit, you'll be fine!

This test focuses on basic numerical calculations and mathematical thinking without tools.

Both the numeracy non-calculator and numeracy calculator tests use similar mathematical concepts including:

♦ Number and algebra

♦ Measurement and geometry

♦ Statistics and probability

You will get a break between the two tests on the day, however, they will both be completed on the same day.

1. Which number is forty thousand eight hundred?

4,800	40,800	4,080	40,080
○	○	○	○

2. Which one of the following shapes is NOT a prism?

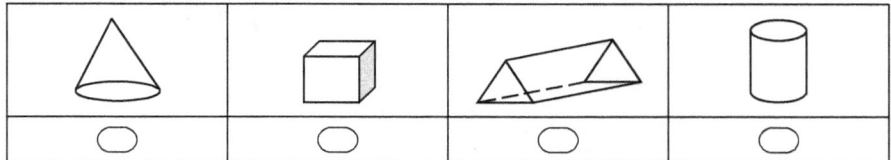

○	○	○	○

3. Which one of the following pictures has the obtuse angle marked?

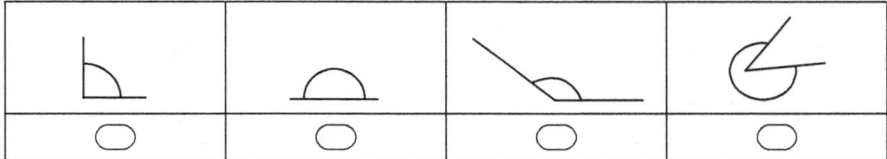

○	○	○	○

4.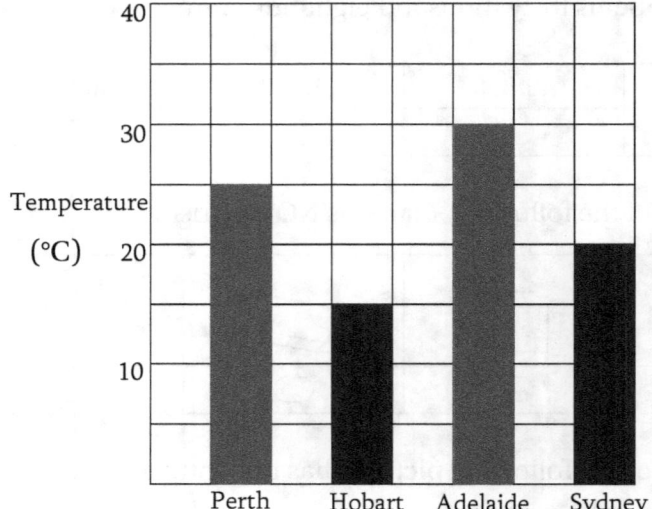

The above graph shows the average January temperatures for different cities in one particular year. In this year what was the average January temperature for Hobart?

12°C	15°C	20°C	25°C
○	○	○	○

5. What is the average (mean) of 11.7, 14.42, 16.84?

13.94	14.14	14.32	14.42
○	○	○	○

6. Which number is exactly halfway between $5\frac{2}{3}$ and $8\frac{1}{3}$

$6\frac{1}{3}$	$6\frac{1}{3}$	7	$7\frac{1}{3}$
○	○	○	○

7.

How many lines of symmetry does the above square have?

2	3	4	6
○	○	○	○

8.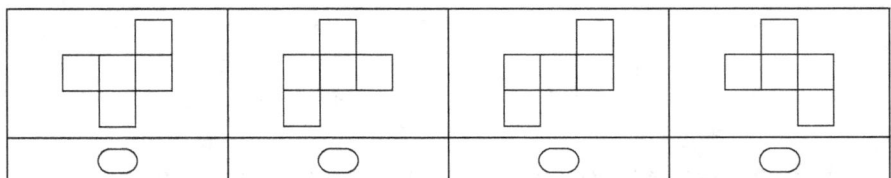

If the above shape is rotated 90° in an anticlockwise direction and then flipped over the line AB, which one of the following shapes would it look like?

○	○	○	○

9. 30 discs coloured green or yellow are placed in a bag so that $\frac{5}{6}$ of the discs are yellow. What is the ratio of green to yellow discs in the bag?

5:6	6:5	1:5	5:1
○	○	○	○

10. If a car uses 12 litres of petrol for every 100 km it travels, how many litres of petrol will the car use to travel 450 km?

L

11.

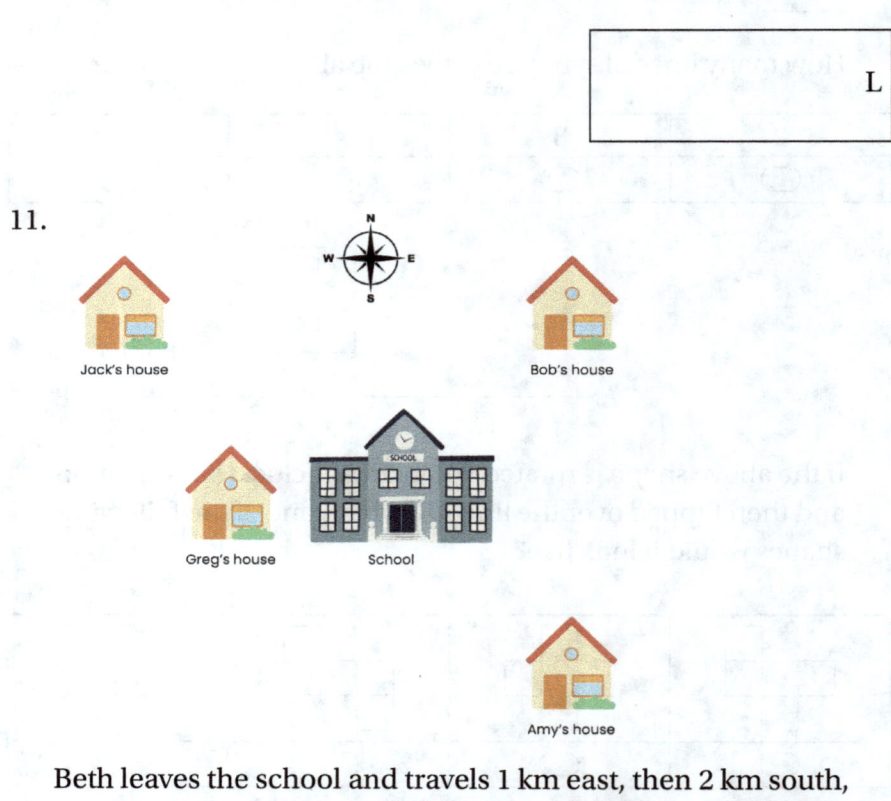

Beth leaves the school and travels 1 km east, then 2 km south, then 3 km west and then 4 km north to arrive at one of the above houses which is the house of her friend. Who is her friend?

Bob	Amy	Greg	Jack
○	○	○	○

12. A cyclist travels 1,500 m in 2 minutes. How fast is the cyclist travelling in km/hr?

km/hr

13. 15 cans of drink are displayed in a shop so that any one layer has one less can than the layer below it. If there is 1 can in the top layer, how many cans will there be in the bottom layer?

14. Which one of the following times is the same as 25 to 10?

9:25	9:35	10:25	10:35
◯	◯	◯	◯

15. How much is needed to increase 4.873 to the nearest whole number?

16. How many quarters are there in $16\frac{1}{2}$?

17.

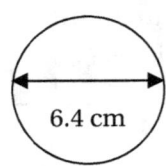
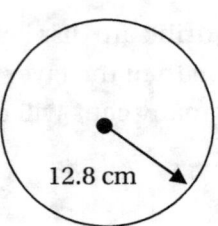

What is the ratio of the circumference of the smaller circle to the larger circle?

8:1	1:8	4:1	1:4
○	○	○	○

18. $\frac{1}{9}$ of Sam's money is $103.

How much money does Sam have altogether?

19. Aaron bought 12 golf balls for $31.56. Marjorie wants to buy 7 of the same type of golf ball.

How much will Marjorie have to pay?

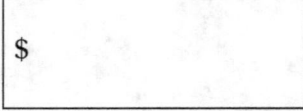

20. Peter left home at 4:20 pm on Thursday and arrived at his destination at 7:14 am on the following day.

How long did his journey take?

hours	mins

21. 25 of the 40 children in Year 8 learn a musical instrument. What percentage of these students learn a musical instrument?

25%	55%	62.5%	65%
○	○	○	○

22.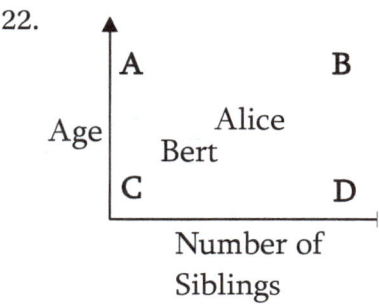

If Richard is older than Alice and has fewer siblings than Bert, then which letter in the above graph represents Richard?

A	B	C	D
○	○	○	○

23.

Ahmed made this large cube using small cubes with a side length of 1 cm. Alan wants to make a large cube the same size as Ahmed's, but he only has cubes with a side length of 2 cm. How many cubes with a side length of 2 cm will Alan need?

8	16	24	32
○	○	○	○

24.

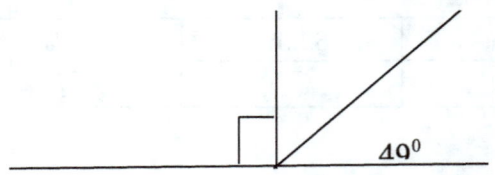

What is the value of x?

25.

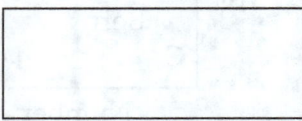

80 students were asked to choose their favourite colour out of red, yellow, green and blue. The above graph shows the results.

How many students chose green?

26. A rectangle has an area of 115 m². If the width of the rectangle is 6.25 m, then what is the length of the rectangle?

m

27.

A bird looking down on the above shape would see which one of the following?

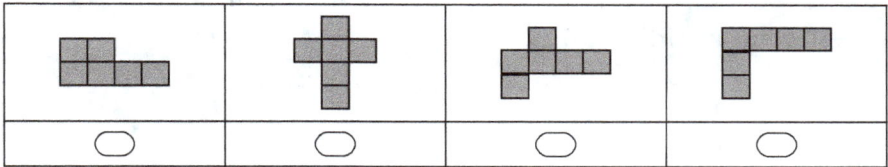

28.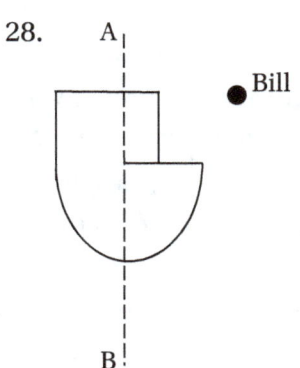

When a mirror is placed along the line AB, which one of the following shapes does Bill see?

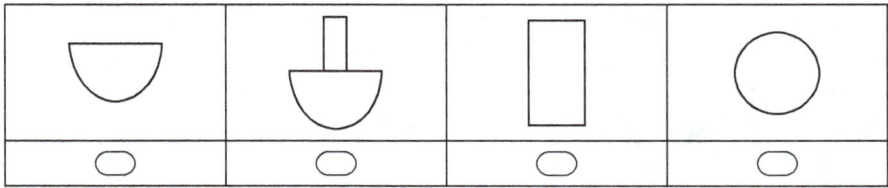

29. What is the answer when 1 metre is added to 3 millimetres?

1.003 m	1.03 m	130 mm	1300 mm
○	○	○	○

30. What are the prime factors of 63?

9×7	$3^2 \times 7$	63×1	$2^3 \times 7$
○	○	○	○

31. 42 Year 6 students at the Learn Well Primary School catch the bus each day. If this is 30% of the Year 6 students, how many students are in Year 6?

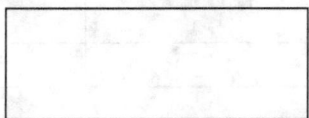

32. Danny has 20 cubes of the same size. He uses them to make four towers by placing cubes, one on top of the other. The first tower is half the height of the third tower. The second tower is the same height as the third tower and the fourth tower is $2\frac{1}{2}$ times the height of the second tower. How many cubes are in the second tower?

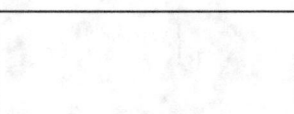

Answers

Writing

Here is a sample writing response for the **Narrative** prompt.

The River

The quest for Thomas was to find the sacred pictures in stone. Then he would be Thomas, the Perfect Knight. His lord told him to follow the big river to where the small river entered.

He began his journey in the early spring. When he reached the big river, the remaining winter mud made the path hard to walk on. At night he would ask for shelter.

"I am a wayfarer on a quest to find the sacred pictures."

Everyone showed him kindness and respect.

Day after day he followed the big river observing the longer hours of daylight, the brighter sun and the green leaves. He wondered how long his journey would take.

The time of two full moons passed. Thomas knew his body was stronger. He felt he could slay dragons and win jousting tournaments, but he needed a sign.

It was the day after he saw the half moon. Thomas heard the water before he saw it. The small river flowed noisily over stones and rocks. As he leaned over to drink, he nearly fell. There, a handspan below the surface on the dark stone, were the sacred pictures.

On the cloth inside his tunic he copied the pictures to prove that he had succeeded in his quest.

He was now Thomas, the Perfect Knight.

Here is a sample writing response for the **Persuasive** prompt.

Every student should play a sport

Because of the enormous benefits obtained from living an active life, I believe that all students should play a sport and particularly, at least one team sport. Besides learning how to play the game, children who participate in team sports develop a sense of belonging and make friends with other members of their team. They learn to get on with students they do not necessarily like. They learn to appreciate the fact that not all people have the same level of skills and abilities, but by working together they can succeed in arriving at a common goal. They learn to communicate with others and to cooperate with them and they learn to respect the umpires and their decisions.

Sport teaches students to be resilient through sharing both positive and negative experiences, as they learn to deal with the excitement of winning and the sadness that accompanies losing a match. Children who play sport are less likely to be bullied as they have the support of their teammates. They learn to be less selfish as they help and support the members of their team.

There are enormous health benefits from participating in team sports. Such activity helps to maintain a healthy body weight, develop good coordination and the endorphins that are released when playing sport help maintain positive mental health. Children get a healthy tiredness from physical activity and, hence, sleep well. There is also evidence that suggests sport played in one's youth can help avoid bone disease in old age.

To participate in the training required for a team sport, students have to be highly organised and practise self-discipline, patience and persistence. These talents can carry over into their academic pursuits. They can help to improve performance in all subjects and are skills that will be helpful during later life in the workforce.

With all these positive effects from playing sport, why would anyone ever suggest that a student and playing sport are not meant for each other?

Reading

Australian drought

1. **Where does grey water come from?**
   - ○ taps
   - ○ rainwater tanks
   - ● washing machines
   - ○ gutters

   ***Washing machines** is the correct answer. Patty's letter tells us this when she states in the second paragraph that people should be using 'grey water from their washing machines.'*

2. **Which of the following do the two writers disagree on?**
   - ○ water needs to be conserved
   - ● the Government is doing enough
   - ○ the environment is precious
   - ○ rainwater tanks help in a drought

   ***The Government is doing enough** is the correct answer. Patty states in her letter that she doesn't think the Government is doing enough. Bill's responding letter argues that the Government has 'put plenty of restrictions on the use of water,' and that people who buy water tanks 'can claim money bank from the Government.' Both these arguments suggest that Bill disagrees with Patty and believes that the Government is doing enough. Also, Bill clearly agrees with Patty on the other points.*

3. **Bill writes that the Government has *'put plenty of restrictions on the use of water'*. Why does he write this?**

    o   he agrees with Patty

    o   he works for the Government

    ●   he disagrees with Patty

    o   he thinks that Australians are water 'Wallys'

    He disagrees with Patty *is the correct answer. Bill's letter is a response to Patty's letter and his comments on the Government are made to show that he disagrees with Patty in her argument that the Government is not doing enough.*

4. **Why does Patty think that water tanks are a great idea?**

    o   so people will use less grey water

    o   so people will use more tap water

    o   so people can get money back from the Government

    ●   so people will use more rainwater

    So people will use more rainwater *is the correct answer. The answers referring to the use of grey water and tap water are both completely incorrect. Only Bill notes that people can claim money from the Government for buying water tanks. Patty does not discuss this point.*

5. **What does Patty's letter tell us about Patty?**
   - ○ that she likes the Government
   - ● that she cares for the environment
   - ○ that she cares for Bill
   - ○ that she is not a farmer

   She cares for the environment *is the correct answer. Patty's letter does not indicate that she likes the Government, and it does not state that she is, or is not, a farmer. Also, Patty's letter was written before Bill's responding letter, suggesting that she did not know Bill at the time she wrote her letter.*

6. **What type of letter is Bill's?**
   - ○ a comment
   - ○ an instruction
   - ● a response
   - ○ a list

   A response *is the best answer. In the first sentence, Bill's letter states that he agrees with Patty's letter on a number of points, therefore, Bill's letter is written as an answer, or response, to Patty's letter.*

Eggs

7. **Why would Thomas have gone up to the chook shed instead of the house?**
   - ○ to get out of the sun
   - ● because his dad wouldn't catch him stealing eggs from there
   - ○ to hide from the narrator
   - ○ for extra eggs

Because his dad wouldn't catch him stealing eggs from there is the correct answer. In the text, the narrator states 'Thomas wouldn't have gone inside for the eggs if his Dad was awake, he would have snuck up back to the chook shed instead.' This suggests that Thomas does not want to be caught stealing eggs by his dad and explains why Thomas would have gone to the chook shed instead.

8. **What does the narrator mean by the sentence '...It will get hot enough'?**

    The narrator means that the sun will heat the tin enough to cook the eggs.

9. **What does '...their clear jelly bodies start to turn a wispy, milky white...' mean?**
    - ○ Thomas and the narrator are turning white
    - ○ the sun is going down
    - ● the eggs are cooking
    - ○ the eggs are rotten

    The eggs are cooking is the correct answer. The 'clear jelly bodies' is a reference to the eggs, which turn white when they are cooked.

10. **In the story, Thomas' dad did a late shift the night before, so Thomas thinks he has until at least three o'clock before he has to go in. This suggests that Thomas**
    - ○ needs to go in before the sun goes down
    - ● needs to go in before his dad wakes up
    - ○ knows that his dad will not be angry
    - ○ will get into trouble if he goes to the chook shed

    That Thomas needs to go in before his dad wakes up is the best answer. In the text, Thomas is guessing that his dad will sleep until at least three because he worked late the night before.

11. **What kind of word best describes the relationship between Thomas and the narrator?**

    ○ brothers
    ○ enemies
    ● friends
    ○ cousins

Friends is the best answer. If Thomas and the narrator were brothers, the narrator would call the man in the story 'Dad' and not 'Thomas' dad'. If the boys in this story were cousins, Thomas' dad would be an uncle to the narrator. The text does not suggest this and the boys are obviously not enemies.

12. **Why do you think the narrator laughs when Thomas shows off his burnt finger?**

    ○ because he is hot
    ○ because he wants Thomas to be hurt
    ○ because he doesn't like Thomas
    ● because he is amazed

Because he is amazed is the best answer. The narrator laughs in response to what he is being shown because he finds it hard to believe.

Water baby

13. **When the starting gun went off, Shane *'cut the water like a knife'*. This means that Shane**

    ○ used a knife to cut the water
    ○ dove into the water roughly
    ● went through the water sharply
    ○ swam very slowly

Went through the water sharply is the correct answer. From reading the text we can tell that Shane did not use an actual knife to cut the water, nor did she dive roughly or swim slowly.

14. **The text states that Shane *'gave herself over to competitive swimming'.* This means that she**
    - ○ gave up going to school
    - ○ gave up her diet
    - ○ brought herself over to the swimming pool
    - ● gave up other activities for swimming

Gave up other activities for swimming is the correct answer. In the same sentence, the text states that Shane 'gave up all other interests and gave herself over to competitive swimming.'

15. **Shane swam open-eyed underwater**
    - ○ during bathtime
    - ● by age three
    - ○ while snorkelling
    - ○ by age five

By age three is the correct answer. The text states: 'Before she was three she could swim underwater at the pool with her eyes open.'

16. **The main purpose of this text is to**
    - ○ instruct
    - ○ criticise
    - ○ argue
    - ● inform

Inform is the correct answer. The text tells us about Shane Gould and her swimming career. It does not criticise or argue or instruct.

17. **Which quote from the text best shows that Shane was very determined to succeed?**

    ○ 'she knew her gift for swimming was special'

    ○ 'she was so confident she'd win'

    ● 'her persistence and single-mindedness paid off'

    ○ 'she loved the water from babyhood'

    Her persistence and single-mindedness paid off *is the best answer. In this context, 'persistence and single-mindedness' have the same meaning as 'very determined'.*

18. **Why did Shane ask for her braces to be removed before the Olympics?**

    ○ because they were slowing her down

    ● because she was confident she was going to win

    ○ because she didn't like her photo being taken

    ○ because she was persistent

    Because she was confident she was going to win *is the best answer. The text states: '...she was so confident that she'd win gold at the Games that she asked her parents if she could have her braces removed just for the competition.'*

The birds have come back

19. **What do you think the writer is trying to show when she describes the kookaburra as laughing 'hollowly'?**

    ○ the kookaburra sounded hollow from far away

    ● the hollow joy of the fires being over

    ○ tat the kookaburra was lonely

    ○ how hot it was

The hollow joy of the fires being over is the correct answer. This is effectively shown by portraying the hollow laughing of the kookaburra while it sits on a charred fence post.

20. **What does the birds' coming back represent?**

    The birds coming back represents hope after the fire.

21. **What word best describes the birds in the first paragraph?**
    - ○ sad
    - ○ devastated
    - ○ hopeful
    - ● elated

    Elated is the best answer. The writer describes the birds laughing and leaping with joy. They are elated.

22. **How does the tone of the piece change in the second paragraph?**

    The tone changes to despair in the second paragraph while the writer describes the aftermath and destruction left by the fires.

23. **Which of the following sentences in the passage best shows the writer's sense of helplessness?**
    - ○ 'white cockatoos screeching'
    - ● 'flames that spread mercilessly'
    - ○ 'they had escaped the flames'
    - ○ 'the north wind roared'

    Flames that spread mercilessly is the best answer. The writer's use of the word, merciless, shows that they were helpless or powerless against the flames.

24. **What does *'swaying in the thermal'* mean?**
    - ○ the birds were cooling down
    - ● the birds were drifting in the heat
    - ○ the valley was barren
    - ○ the birds were being baked

    ***The birds were drifting in the heat** is the correct answer. The words 'swaying' and 'drifting' are similar in meaning, as are the words 'heat' and 'thermal'.*

Ned Kelly: Black Snake

25. **In *Ned Kelly: Black Snake*, why might the author have opened each chapter with a *'fictionalised recount'*?**
    - ○ it shows Ned Kelly as the terrible villain he was
    - ● to tell the *story* of Ned Kelly as well as the *history* of Ned Kelly
    - ○ there was not enough accurate information available
    - ○ it allows the reader to make their own decisions

    ***To tell the story of Ned Kelly as well as the history of Ned Kelly** is the best answer. The writer is using the fictionalised recounts as a means of giving a true history of Ned Kelly in a story format.*

26. **Which sentence best suggests that *Ned Kelly: Black Snake* reveals more about Ned Kelly than other books about the outlaw?**
    - ○ *'...supported by archival photographs'*
    - ● *'...offers insight into the life of the outlaw'*
    - ○ *'...recounts Kelly's life from his birth'*
    - ○ *'...quotes from correspondence'*

    ***Offers insight into the life of the outlaw** is the best answer. The word 'insight' can be defined as revealing hidden information. The reviewer states that Black Snake offers insight into the life* *of the outlaw, meaning more information is revealed about the outlaw.*

27. **'This is not a glorification of a criminal career' – what does this mean?**

    It means that the writer does not portray Ned Kelly's criminal career as something to be admired or glorified.

28. **The *main* purpose of this review is to**
    - ○ inform the reader about Ned Kelly's history
    - ○ inform the reader about the author, Carole Wilkinson
    - ● recommend *Black Snake* for reading
    - ○ explain that this book is different from other histories of Ned Kelly

    ***Recommend Black Snake for reading** is the best answer. The review is very positive and clearly shows that the reviewer feels the book is worth reading. While the actual book is about Ned Kelly's history, the review itself does not inform the reader about Ned Kelly's history. Nor does the review give much information about the author apart from the manner in which she has written Black Snake. To explain that this book is different from other histories of Ned Kelly is only a small part of the review and not the main purpose.*

29. **This review is**
    - ○ a criticism
    - ○ an argument
    - ○ a comment
    - ● an analysis

    ***An analysis** is the correct answer. The review is an examination of Black Snake that provides more than a simple comment on the book. It is not a criticism of the book or the writer, and it is not an argument putting forth a 'stance' or 'case' on an issue.*

Should we abolish zoos?

30. **What is Big Brother's main argument?**
    - ○ animals make an important contribution to education
    - ○ animals are protected by laws on cruelty
    - ○ modern zoos are animal friendly
    - ● zoos make an important contribution to species preservation

    ***Zoos make an important contribution to species preservation** is the correct answer. The main focus of Big Brother's argument is that zoos play an important part in the survival of endangered species.*

31. **JaneyB refers to zoos as *'some manufactured setting'.* What is the tone of this argument?**
    - ○ joking
    - ● critical
    - ○ practical
    - ○ approving

    ***Critical** is the correct answer. JaneyB is clearly against animals being kept in a manufactured setting.*

32. **What are they all likely to agree on?**
    - ○ modern zoos are different to zoos of old
    - ● animals should be protected
    - ○ zoos are restricted by laws
    - ○ all animals are better off in the wild

    ***Animals should be protected** is the best answer. All the writers in this forum show, through their arguments, that they each care for animals despite their differing opinions on zoos.*

33. **JaneyB argues that zoos give humans an *'artificial impression'.* What she means is that**

    ○ animals in the wild are better off

    ○ only humans benefit from the existence of zoos

    ● animals do not behave realistically in the zoo

    ○ animals in the zoo are artificial

Animals do not behave realistically in the zoo is the best answer. Though JaneyB is likely to agree with most of the answers, the question is asking us what JaneyB means when she talks about animals in the zoo giving an 'artificial impression'.

34. **In her first comment, what is JaneyB's main concern?**

    ○ zoos are not educational

    ○ zoos are not realistic

    ● zoos keep animals away from their real homes

    ○ zoos are environmentally unfriendly

Zoos keep animals away from their real homes is the correct answer. The question refers specifically to JaneyB's first comment, in which she states that it is 'not fair to keep animals in such small spaces that are nothing like their real homes'.

35. **Spaceman argues the only difference between zoo habitats and wild habitats is that *'there are no predators'*. This means that**

    ○ zoos only keep animals that aren't predators

    ● zoos ensure that the animals can't hurt one another

    ○ humans can view the animals safely

    ○ wild habitats are better

Zoos ensure that the animals can't hurt one another is the best answer. A predator is an animal that preys on another. Zoos still have animals that are predators, but they are kept in habitats in which they cannot prey on other animals.

36. **What effect might this lack of predators have on the animals?**

   It would likely cause the animals to behave differently because they do not have to hunt for food or protect themselves against predators.

Greetings from Luanda, Angola

37. **In the first paragraph, Luanda is portrayed as**
    - ○ a desolate landscape
    - ● a place undergoing development
    - ○ a large, bustling city
    - ○ a drab-grey cement city

   A place undergoing development is the best answer. The first paragraph is dedicated to describing all the building, landscaping and road works occurring in Luanda.

38. **Why do you think the third paragraph is written in the form of a story?**
    - ○ so that the writing does not become monotonous
    - ○ to ensure that the reader is concentrating
    - ○ to make the scene shorter
    - ● to show the reader how the poverty in Luanda affects the writer

   To show the reader how the poverty in Luanda affects the writer is the best answer. This paragraph is written just after the writer talks of the poverty in Luanda; it is written this way to highlight the poverty and how it affects the writer.

39. *'...this year there seems to be more trees, decorations and "things to buy" than there were last year.'* **What does this suggest?**

   ○ Christmas is becoming more popular in Luanda

   ○ the President's mother likes Christmas trees

   ● Luanda is becoming more prosperous

   ○ the writer is beginning to like Luanda

   Luanda is becoming more prosperous *is the best answer. Much of the letter is dedicated to describing the progress of Luanda, its development and the greater availability of goods.*

40. *'There's greater variety of goods for sale and an election, the first for nearly two decades, has brought some hope.'* **What might they be hoping for?**

   ● less poverty

   ○ to leave Luanda

   ○ more Christmas merchandise

   ○ more markets

   Less poverty *is the best answer. The greater variety of goods for sale and an election are signs of a developing nation. Development can lead to less poverty. The writer gives no indication she wishes to leave Luanda.*

41. **Why does the writer change her mind and buy a pineapple?**

   Because she realises that the lady has a small child to feed and is pregnant with another child. Selling the fruit is the lady's livelihood. The writer feels compelled to help her.

Language conventions

Spelling

Each sentence has one word that is incorrectly spelt. Write the correct spelling of the word in the box.

1. We need to show caushun when crossing the road.

   | caution |

2. I am very good at rapping presents.

   | wrapping |

3. The mountain's summit was at a great hite.

   | height |

4. The art galery has many famous paintings.

   | gallery |

5. Tim ran the cross-country course energeticly.

   | energetically |

6. The tourist lost his luggidge at the airport.

   | luggage |

7. The fan wanted the celebrity's autograf.

   | autograph |

8. It is rude to talk with a mouthfull of food. | mouthful

9. Sientists will soon discover a cure for cancer. | scientists

10. Professor Jones studied the dinosaur fossel. | fossil

11. The cathedral was visited as a holey shrine. | holy

12. The hospital pashent was recovering from her injuries. | patient

13. You will find my letter inclosed in the package. | enclosed

14. It is important to do some streching before exercise. | stretching

The spelling mistakes in these sentences have been circled. Write the correct spelling for each circled word in the box.

15. Jack showed his (strenth) when he carried

    strength

16. that heavy sack of (potatos) all the way home.

    potatoes

17. Everyone comments on how (musculer)

    muscular

18. he is, but it was still very (impresive.)

    impressive.

19. He appears so (distrest) every time

    distressed

20. I make any (atempt) to

    attempt

21. (approche) him that I'm not

    approach

22. sure how to (acheeve) it.

    achieve

23. He wore a (disgize) that was

| 23. disguise |

24. so (efective) that not even his

| 24. effective |

25. own family could (gess) who he was.

| 25. guess |

Grammar and punctuation

26. Which of the following correctly completes the sentence?

> You can travel more _____ by train than you can by car.

quick	quicker	quickest	quickly
○	○	○	●

27. Which of the following correctly completes the sentence?

> Dora went to bed early last night because she _____ tired.

have	is	was	were
○	○	●	○

28. Shade one bubble to show where the missing apostrophe (') should go.

Mark looked for the dogs lead so that his sisters could take the dog for a walk.

29. Which of the following correctly completes the sentence?

> Prince William, _____ is heir to the throne, is a good horse rider.

that	which	when	who
○	○	○	●

30. Which of the following correctly completes the sentence?

The book, _____ was green, belonged to the library.

who	what	which	why
○	○	●	○

31. Which sentence is correct?

○ I and Jane is very good at playing tennis.

○ Me and Jane are very good at playing tennis.

○ Jane and me is very good at playing tennis.

● Jane and I are very good at playing tennis.

32. Which of the following correctly completes the sentence?

The use of herbs and spices in cooking _____ on the increase in Australia.

is	are	am	were
●	○	○	○

33. Which of the following correctly completes the sentences?

Karen is very tall. _____, her older brother is quite short.

So	Therefore	However	Because
○	○	●	○

34. Which sentence has the correct punctuation?

- ● He asked for it politely, so I let him have it.
- ○ He asked "for it politely," so, I let him have it.
- ○ He asked for "it politely" so I let him, have it.
- ○ He asked, "for it politely, so I let him", have it.

35. Which of the following correctly completes the sentence?

They bought tickets that allowed them to sit the _____ to the stage.

more closest	closest	closely	more closer
○	●	○	○

36. Which of the following correctly completes the sentence?

The kangaroo and the koala are native _____ Australia.

for	with	in	to
○	○	○	●

37. Which of the following correctly completes the sentence?

They _____ driven slower in the rain.

should of	should'ave	should've	shouldve
○	○	●	○

38. Which of the following correctly completes the sentence?

> The restaurant had an _____ atmosphere that attracted customers.

vibrant	warm	alluring	joyful
○	○	●	○

39. Shade **two** bubbles to show where the missing commas (,) should go.

> I enjoy eating fish and chips and I enjoy eating chocolate
> ○   ●   ○
>
> but I wouldn't enjoy eating them together.
> ○

40. Which sentence is correct?

● They were gathering them up and sorting them into pairs.

○ They gathered them up and sorting them into pairs.

○ They were gathering them up and were sorted them into pairs.

○ They gathered them and sort them into pairs.

41. Which of the following correctly completes the sentence?

> He drove the car _____ .

extremely quickly	extreme quick	extreme quickly	extremely quick
●	○	○	○

42. Which of the following correctly completes the sentence?

Madeline decided _____ a new laptop computer.

on buying	in buying	buying	to buying
●	○	○	○

43. Which of the following correctly completes the sentence?

Some people prefer savoury food _____ sweet food.

from	than	to	for
○	○	●	○

44. Shade one bubble to show where the missing apostrophe (') should go.

○   ●   ○   ○

The girls really admired Amys new shoes made from crocodile skins.

45. Which sentence has the correct punctuation?

○ Suddenly a large bird swooped down swallowed a bug and flew off.

● Suddenly, a large bird swooped down, swallowed a bug, and flew off.

○ Suddenly a large bird, swooped down, swallowed a bug, and flew off.

○ Suddenly a large bird swooped down, swallowed a bug and, flew off.

46. Which sentence has the correct punctuation?

- ● The bats' wings, all flapping together, sounded like thunder.
- ○ The bat's wings, all flapping together, sounded like thunder.
- ○ The bats, wings all flapping together sounded, like thunder.
- ○ The bats' wing's all flapping, together sounded like thunder.

47. Which sentence is correct?

- ● Lucy and Anne were still hungry even though they had eaten lunch.
- ○ Lucy and Anne were still hungry even though she has eaten lunch.
- ○ Lucy and Anne are still hungry even though they eaten lunch.
- ○ Lucy and Anne is still hungry even though they had eaten lunch.

48. Which of the following correctly completes the sentence?

Do you have a table _____ can seat thirteen?

who	that	what	and
○	●	○	○

49. Which sentence has the correct punctuation?
    - ○ My brother will be in New Zealand on christmas day.
    - ○ my brother will be in New zealand on Christmas Day.
    - ○ My Brother will be in New Zealand on Christmas Day.
    - ● My brother will be in New Zealand on Christmas Day.

50. Which sentence has the correct punctuation?
    - ○ as she left for work Chloe called to Tegan, "See you later".
    - ● As she left for work, Chloe called to Tegan, "See you later".
    - ○ As she left for work, Chloe called to Tegan "see you later".
    - ○ As she left for work, chloe called to tegan, "see you later".

Language conventions answers in detail

Questions 1–25 are spelling mistakes.

Question 26: The adverbial form *quickly* is the only appropriate one to modify the verb *travel*. The other options are adjectives.

Question 27: The simple past tense singular *was* is the most appropriate answer because it refers to a single incident that was completed in the past. The two answers using the present does not agree, and *were* is plural.

Question 28: The lead belongs grammatically to the dog, and so requires a singular possessive inflection: 's.

Question 29: Prince William is a person, so the sentence requires the relative pronoun 'who'.

Question 30: A relative pronoun is required here, so 'what' and 'why' (interrogative pronouns) cannot be used, and 'who' is used to refer to people, so 'which' is the only correct answer.

Question 31: The first person pronoun as a subject is 'I'. 'I' has been used with *Jane* to form a plural subject. The subject-verb agreement when the subject is *Jane and I* requires the verb 'to be' to take the plural form 'are'.

Question 32: This is subject-verb agreement. 'The use' is the noun phrase (post-modified with 'of herbs and spices'). It is third person singular and must therefore take the verb 'is'. 'Am' is first person; 'are' and 'were' are either second person or third person plural.

Question 33: 'So', 'because' and 'therefore' all suggest cause and effect, and it would be unusual to find a subordinating conjunction to connect these two clauses as neither clause is subordinate. The adverbial 'however' allows the second clause to modify the content of the first clause.

Question 34: There is no speech directly reported in this sentence, so there is no need for speech marks. The only sentence without speech marks is: *He asked for it politely, so I let him have it.*

Question 35: The use of the definite article 'the' indicates the missing word has to be *closest* because it is the only one that can function as a noun phrase in this context. *Closely* is an adverb that cannot be preceded by *the*, and *more closer* and *most closest* are double comparative and double superlative adjectival phrases respectively.

Question 36: The preposition *to* is the only appropriate option to complete the verb phrase in Standard English.

Question 37: The phrase being contracted is 'should have', which is *should've*.

Question 38: The adjective to follow the indefinite article *an* has to begin with a vowel.

Question 39: The commas are used to separate the clause elements. The first one comes before the coordinating conjunction *and*, and the second one before the conjunction *but*. (The first conjunction *and* does not coordinate clauses, but rather is used to list.)

Question 40: The verb tenses and aspects have to agree in a compound sentence. The use of the past progressive tense *were gathering* in the first clause requires the need of the gerund *sorting* in the second clause. Also, the gerund or present tense cannot be used in the second clause if the simple past had been used in the first.

Question 41: The appropriate phrase has to feature two adverbs. The first adverb *extremely* is used to modify the adverb *quickly*, which has been used to modify the verb *drove*.

Question 42: The only phrase that fits is the verb phrase *on buying* in Standard English in this context.

Question 43: *To* is the only appropriate preposition in forming such a comparison in Standard English.

Question 44: The *shoes* belong grammatically to *Amy*, so a singular possessive inflection: 's is required (*Amy's*).

Question 45: The sentence begins with a capital letter and ends with a full stop. There is a comma after the adverbial *suddenly*, and in the compound sentence, a comma is used to mark each of the three clauses: *a large bird swooped down* and *swallowed a bug* and *and flew off*.

Question 46: The *wings* belong grammatically to the *bats*, so a plural possessive inflection (') is required on *bats* ('bats'). There is also a comma identifying the embedded clause 'all flapping together', and the sentence begins with a capital letter and ends with a full stop.

Question 47: To make sense, each clause had to have a subject-verb agreement, as well as an agreement in verb tense. Only the sentence: 'Lucy and Anne were still hungry even though they had eaten lunch' achieves this.

Question 48: This is a single clause and as such, the relative pronoun 'that' is required to modify the noun table. 'Who' refers to people and would signal a relative clause, 'and' is a conjunction, and 'what' is an interrogative pronoun.

Question 49: The sentence begins with a capital letter, and all proper nouns are similarly given capital letters. *Christmas Day* and *New Zealand* are proper nouns, *brother* is not.

Question 50: The sentence begins with a capital letter and ends with a full stop. The adverbial clause 'as she left for work' has a comma to separate it. In writing speech, there needs to be a comma before the speech marks, the first word of the utterance needs a capital letter, followed by speech marks to close the utterance.

Numeracy non-calculator

1. $9 \times 8 = 72$, $6 \times 12 = 72$, so missing number is **12**
2. A vertex is where 2 adjacent lines meet to form a corner or an angle. There is only **1** vertex in this diagram.
3. $5^2 = \mathbf{5 \times 5}$
4. 6 on the x axis up to 3 on the y axis gives the **gum** tree.
5. It is possible but not likely for Josie to get a white marble since there is 1 white marble in the box. Hence, it is not certain she will get a black one. The true statement is that **it is unlikely that Josie will select a white marble.**
6. The small hand is on 8, so 8 o'clock. The large hand is on 2, i.e. 2 lots of 5 is 10 minutes after 8. **8:10**
7. Each number is 6 less than the number before it. Missing number is $88 - 6 = \mathbf{82}$
8. A horizontal line through X produces a mirror image. A vertical line through M and W produces a mirror image. Hence **P** does not have a line of symmetry.
9. $0.03 \times 100 = \mathbf{3\%}$
10. Amy stayed at her friend's house from 12:20 till 12:40, not an hour. Amy arrived at her friend's house at 12:20, so took 20 minutes. Amy rode home from 12:40 till 1:00, which is **20 minutes to ride home**.
11. Distance around the fence $= 40 \times 5 = 200$. 5 times around the fence
    $= 200 \times 5 = \mathbf{1{,}000m}$
12. Perimeter $= 5 + 10 + 12 + 4 + 7 + 6 = \mathbf{44\ cm}$
13. **1** is the smallest. All the other numbers have a bit added onto 1
14. $6.45 \div 3 = 2.15$. $2 \times 2.15 = \mathbf{\$4.30}$
15. 526 is between 520 and 530. It is 6 from 520 and 4 from 530 so it is closest to **530**

16. $\frac{1}{8}$ of 24 = 3, so $\frac{3}{8}$ of 24 = 3 × 3 = **9**

17. 25 minutes before 4:15 is 10 minutes before 4:00 i.e. **3:50**

18. There are 4 green sections out of a total of 8 sections.

    Chance of green is 4:8 = **1:2**

19. 2 × 3 + (8 − 5) ÷ 3 = 2 × 3 + 3 ÷ 3 = 2 × 3 + 1 = 6 + 1 = **7**

20. Anne gets 3 portions and Ben gets 1 portion.

    This is a total of 4 portions. 60 ÷ 4 = 15

    Ben gets $15 and Anne gets $45

21. 33 ÷ 22 = 1 and remainder 11. $1\frac{11}{22} = 1\frac{1}{2}$

22. X is the base. D comes up as a side and E wraps around to form another side. B comes up as a side and C wraps around to form another side. A folds across as the top. Hence, **A is opposite X.**

23. **South-west**

24. 1.25 + 0.035 = **1.285 L**

25. 360 − 25 = **335°**

26. $\frac{3}{5} + \frac{1}{10} = \frac{6}{10} + \frac{1}{10} = \frac{7}{10}$

    $1\frac{1}{2} - \frac{7}{10} = \frac{15}{10} - \frac{7}{10} = \frac{8}{10} = \frac{4}{5}$

27. 25 + 32 = **57**

28. $\frac{76}{100} \times \frac{50}{1} = \frac{76}{2} = 38$

29. Con is 6 m from behind Alex and 11 m from the tree, so Alex is 5 m from the tree. Bridie is 9 m from the tree, so Bridie is **4 m** behind Alex.

30. 8.4 ÷ 0.4 = 84 ÷ 4 = **21**

31. 6 apricots = 2 oranges = 3 apples, so **1 apple = 2 apricots**

32. When the paper is folded it will look like **the second answer from the left**.

Numeracy calcluator

1. **40,800**

2. **The first answer on the left** is not a prism as you cannot cut equal parallel slices through it.

3. An obtuse angle is between 90º and 180º, so **the third answer from the left**.

4. The Hobart rectangle comes to a height of **15ºC**

5. $(11.7 + 14.42 + 16.84) \div 3 = \mathbf{14.32}$

6. $\left(5\frac{2}{3} + 8\frac{1}{3}\right) \div 2 = 7$

7. 2 diagonals, a vertical line through the middle and a horizontal line through the middle. **4**

8. **Second answer from the left**

9. G:Y $\frac{1}{6} : \frac{5}{6}$ = **1:5**

10. Number of 100s in 450 = 4.5, so number of litres of petrol = 4.5 × 12 = **54 L**

11. 1 east and 3 west means she ends up west of the school. 2 south and 4 north means she ends up north of the school. **Jack is her friend.**

12. 1,500 m in 2 min. 30 ×1,500 m = 45,000 m in 1 hour = **45 km/hr**

13. 1 + 2 + 3 + 4 + 5 = 15 so **5** in the bottom layer

14. **9:35**

15. 5 − 4.873 = **0.127**

16. 4 quarters in 1 so 16 × 4 = 64 quarters in 16 plus 2 quarters in a half

    = **66 quarters** in $16\frac{1}{2}$

17. C (for small circle) = π × D = 6.4π
    C (for large circle) = π × D = 25.6π
    Ratio: 6.4π:25.6π = **1:4**

18. $\frac{1}{9} = 103, \frac{9}{9} = 103 \times 9 = \$927$

19. Cost of 1 golf ball = 31.56 ÷ 12 = 2.63
    Cost of 7 golf balls = 2.63 × 7 = **$18.41**

20. 4:20 pm till 4:20 am is 12 hours. There are another 3 hours till 7:20 am, i.e. 15 hours. Trip finished at 7:14 am, i.e. 6 minutes less, so **14 hours 54 minutes**.

21. $\frac{25}{40} \times \frac{100}{1} = 62.5\%$

22. Older than Alice means A or B. Fewer siblings than Bert means A or C.

    Hence, Richard is **A**.

23. Ahmed uses 4 × 4 × 4 = 64 cubes.

    Every one of Alan's cubes covers 8 of Ahmed's.

    64 ÷ 8 = **8**

24. $x = 90 - 49 = \mathbf{41}$

25. $\frac{1}{4} \times 80 = 20$

26. Length = 115 ÷ 6.25 = **18.4 m**

27. **The last of the alternative answers.**

28. **The second from the left of the alternative answers.**

29. 1,003 millimetres or **1.003 m**

30. 1, 9 and 63 are not prime numbers. $2^3 \times 7 \neq 63$, so $\mathbf{3^2 \times 7}$

31. 30% = 42
    $1\% = \frac{42}{30}$
    $100\% = \frac{42}{30} \times 100 = \mathbf{140}$

32. $\frac{x}{2} + x + x + 2\frac{1}{2}x = 20$
    $5x = 20$
    $x = \mathbf{4}$

www.ingramcontent.com/pod-product-compliance
Lightning Source LLC
Chambersburg PA
CBHW050300120526
44590CB00016B/2431